Leadership
Under
Pressure

"The ultimate reward for the leader of people is to be able to say, 'I saw someone grow today, and I helped.'"

"Intensity (goal, focus, and action) + Enthusiasm (expectancy of better things to come) = Charisma."

"The managerial moment of truth comes when you realize that, as the leader, you are the trigger for change in your organization."

Leadership
Under
Pressure

✔ *24 Lessons in High*
Performance Management

DANNY COX
WITH JOHN HOOVER

MCGRAW-HILL
New York Chicago San Francisco Lisbon
London Madrid Mexico City Milan New Delhi
San Juan Seoul Singapore Sydney Toronto

Leadership Under Pressure: 24 lessons in high performance
management

Danny Cox with John Hoover

ISBN 13: 978- 0-07711730-6
ISBN 10: 0-07-711730-1

 **Professional**

Published by:
McGraw-Hill Publishing Company
Shoppenhangers Road,
Maidenhead,
Berkshire, England, SL6 2QL
Telephone: 44 (0) 1628 502500
Fax: 44 (0) 1628 770224
Website: www.mcgraw-hill.co.uk

British Library Cataloguing-in-Publication Data
A catalogue record of this book is available from the British Library.

McGraw-Hill books are available at special quantity discounts. Please
contact the corporate sales executive.

Contents

Leadership Under Pressure

☑ Leadership Under Pressure

Only a few feet separate the lead pilot's tailpipe from the nose of my supersonic fighter as we rip through the sky at speeds in excess of 500 miles per hour. I feel the blast from his engine vibrating through my feet on the rudder pedals and through my right hand on the control stick. There are seven more jets behind me packed just as tight in our nine-ship formation.

Almost with one motion, the nose of each fighter gently drops below the horizon. The airspeed builds until the lead pilot pulls back on the stick. The nose of every fighter rises in perfect symmetry as the G forces build. I feel the blood being forced into my legs and feet. All nine of us are now experiencing the same 5 G force—five times our body weight. We tighten our leg and abdominal muscles to keep blood in our upper extremities to avoid blacking out.

I concentrate on keeping my hand on the throttle. If it slips off, the G force will push it down between the side panel and my ejection seat. I will lose my ability to make minor throttle adjustments and hold precise position. As we curve over the top of our perfect loop, the world switches places with the sky. The G forces diminish down the backside. I steal a millisecond glance at the two rearview mirrors. Everyone is still tucked in tight. The G pressure builds again as our lead pilot pulls the nose back up to level flight and eight pilots follow in perfect unison.

The lead pilot takes us through a series of horizon tumbling rolls followed by a formation shift to a nine-ship diamond. It's my turn to fly center position as we make a high-speed, low-level pass over the airfield. The noise of eight other jets in front and back and on both sides, flying two to three yards from wingtip to wingtip, is deafening. It's high-performance flying right to the edge. There's only one word to describe it: *exhilarating*. Wow! How I love it!

It's the ultimate team experience. The difference between life and death can be how well we learn from our successes *and* failures. Our synergy comes from courage, creativity, and being there for each other, no matter what. After leaving the Air force and entering the corporate world, I had to transfer the principles of individual and team high performance to new challenges.

I had to make some tremendous adjustments, but my drive to again be a part of a high-performance team was strong. I sought out advice from the most successful people I could find in various industries. What they taught me, along with some innovations of my own, put my new team into a supersonic climb. In five years, we increased production 800%, morale soared, and turnover dropped to nearly zero.

Consider this your supersonic flight plan as you discover how my team broke the old records and continued to break the new ones. You're going to find out how to become the lead pilot for your team and a barrier-breaking leader.

☑ Use problems to enhance your career

I've broken the sound barrier over 2,000 times at the controls of everything from the F-86 Sabre and the F-102 Delta Dagger to the F-101 Voodoo and the F-16 Viper. I have knocked off a lot of plaster and broken countless windows. My extra duty job in the Air Force was to speak to groups of upset, hostile civilians and convince them that those sonic booms were "the sound of freedom."

Having built a reputation in the military as the "sonic boom salesman," I got into sales when I stopped flying. Those hostile audiences must have provided excellent training, because the transition went smoothly. I did so well in my first year as a salesperson that the company executives asked me to manage one of the sales offices.

I managed that small office for a year with some success. One year later, the same executives showed up again to promote me to manager of the top office in the 36-office chain.

That's when I started making the same mistakes nearly every manager makes. I urged my people not to think of me as their boss, but as a friend who was always right. My goal was to turn everyone in that office into a copy of *me*.

It made perfect sense at the time. Turning the salespeople into Danny Cox clones seemed to be what my bosses wanted to do. If I could get my salespeople to do the job exactly as I had done it, they wouldn't bring me any problems that I hadn't already solved.

Under my management, the number-one office plummeted to number 36 out of 36. One day, as I was trying to figure out the problem, my boss showed up in my office, unannounced, without his usual smile and pleasant demeanor.

"Cox," he said through clenched teeth. "I can now see that it was a mistake making you the manager of this office and I feel it's only fair to tell you that I'm already looking for your replacement.

That was the shortest and the most *effective* motivational seminar I ever attended. I needed to learn how to lead—and I needed to learn *fast*.

I sought out the counsel of many successful people and soon learned that I needed to work on myself, not the salespeople. Salespeople get better right after their manager.

The techniques I began using had such an immediate effect that within two weeks my boss stopped looking for a replacement. We were heading back to number one.

Here are three ways you can start turning problems into opportunities:

Think of a problem in the past that turned out to be a positive.

Choose a problem that you can turn into a positive if you apply the right attitude and plan.

Decide on one thing you can do in the next 24 hours to improve your leadership style.

"High performance is often the result of a sudden change in direction."

☐ ~~Accept your limitations~~

☑ Lift your limitations

After returning to the top position, our office leveled off in production amazingly exactly where we had been when I took over. Once we returned to our previous level of performance, we went no further: We unknowingly reached our *self-imposed* barrier.

I emphasize the word "self" because the barriers are not imposed by the company or customers. A self-imposed barrier is nothing more than the dividing line between developed and undeveloped potential. Yet, we look at that line as though it's a wall. Self-imposed barriers are not walls around our lives. They are the margins of our lives where nothing has been written—yet.

Imagine what the world would be like if explorers throughout history believed that they couldn't go anywhere for the first time. That's what we were up against after my office was back at number one. Pushing production higher than ever before meant venturing into uncharted territory. We had reached the collective personal barriers of the team.

My people were not slouches. They were the best in the company and would have been the best in any company. We were already receiving monthly awards for being the top office. Success became a barrier for us. Walt Disney is remembered to this day throughout the Disney organization for warning his staff against resting on their laurels. Ralph Waldo Emerson put it even more profoundly when he said, "A great man is always willing to be little. Whilst he sits on the cushion of advantages, he goes to sleep."

Another great executive once said to me, "Good is the enemy of best and best is the enemy of better." When most people get to be good, they start to think, "What's the point of struggling to be best? Isn't good good enough?"

I challenged my team to break through their personal production records and they responded. I asked them to focus on their own records on a daily, weekly, monthly, quarterly, yearly basis, instead of other people's records. When they did, energy, morale, and production skyrocketed.

As our performance received increasing acclamation and overall attention, I was asked where I got all of those great people and how I built such a record-breaking team. Did I steal top producers from our competition or recruit at the top business schools? The one-word answer was "No." They were just ordinary people who discovered they could do the most extraordinary things with their newly discovered potential.

Here are some things you can do right now to help develop undeveloped potential in your team:

Meet individually with your key people to set goals: Tell them, "Don't worry about breaking anyone else's personal record. Just think about breaking your own record on a daily, weekly, monthly, quarterly, and yearly basis."

Monitor each team member's progress continuously: Help that person stay focused.

Celebrate record-breaking performances: Do this on a regular basis to show your support and appreciation for your team's effort.

"Accomplishment is your birthright. Limitations are adopted."

☐ Hope for a miracle

☑ Search for what works

I love it when people fight against incredible odds to triumph over problems. Dr. Norman Vincent Peale once said, "You're only as big as the problem that stops you." I am thankful for men and women who were bigger than the problems that would have stopped and did stop so many others. The *world* got better right after *they* got better.

During the dark hours when my boss was out looking for my replacement, I started reading articles about successful people in newspapers and magazines. When I came across someone local, I called the person and said, "You don't know me, but my name is Danny Cox and I've just destroyed the number-one office in my company by taking it from first place to 36th in three months. My boss is looking for my replacement right now. Can I have lunch with you?"

These successful people not only took my calls, buy agreed to have lunch with me. Some sensed the urgency in my voice; others just wanted to meet the person who could single-handedly wreak havoc on an entire organization. The one quality in every one of these success stories was an entrepreneurial spirit. Each saw me as a challenge—or at least a curiosity.

I listened and learned and immediately started applying the lessons. I have never stopped seeking out the advice and counsel of effective leaders. Take someone to lunch before someone else eats yours. Pay attention to what's happening in your organization, your industry, and your local business community, so you can learn without experiencing your own disasters.

Work on yourself first. Your pursuit of excellence will set the agenda for everyone in your organization. Just before you drift off to sleep, ask yourself, "Who am I *impressing* . . . ?" When people are impressed, they say, "You do good work." When they're *inspired*, they say, "I wish I did my work as well as you do yours."

You must lead by your example of excellence. Think of it this way: somebody somewhere is going to get better because you're reading this book.

Here are some ways to start your pursuit of excellence:

Learn from leaders around you: List the three people you admire most within your organization and the three you admire most outside of your organization. They should be accessible to you. Take these people individually to lunch or, at least, talk with them about their secrets to successful leadership. They'll enjoy telling you.

Put those methods and techniques to work: Apply what you learn to your leadership challenges. Give your benefactors feedback on how their methods and techniques work for you—and tell them about any innovations you come up with.

Focus on inspiring rather than impressing: When you impress, you rise above others. When you inspire, you bring them up with you.

"To achieve great things, know more than the average person considers necessary."

☐ ~~Settle for who you are~~

☑ **Develop characteristics of great leaders**

Here is a list of 10 characteristics that are common in high-performing leaders. They do not come naturally. Great leaders develop them. The characteristics of great leaders are universal and timeless. They reflect what leaders choose to believe and how they decide to behave. Great leaders demonstrate all 10 characteristics—regardless of their field.

1. *Uncompromising integrity:* It's the foundation for quality and service to both internal and external customers. The would-be leader who doesn't have this will be a "flash in the pan."

2. *Absence of pettiness:* The greatest drain of energy in an organization is pettiness. Eliminating it results in high energy. Leaders understand the difference between interesting and important.

3. *Works on things by priority:* This results in stability under pressure and makes for an excellent problem solver. A leader who works by priorities prepares a daily priority list: he or she starts with #1 and doesn't deal with #2 when finished, but instead deals with the new #1, and so on.

4. *Courageous:* Leaders don't lead life meekly, they know there is a deep well of courage within each of us, whether or not we use it. Leaders do what they fear to keep fear from taking charge. Their credo is "It's always too soon to quit!"

5. *Committed:* Leaders know that they won't die an early death by working hard in a job they love. They never hear low achievers saying, "Slow down! You're going to ruin your health!" Their work is a developed art form.

6. *Goal oriented:* Focus is the antidote for pain in the accomplishment of stellar goals. Leaders understand that a lack of goals starts the process of both physical and mental shutdown.

7. *Unorthodox:* These are the creators, the innovators, and the think-outside-the-box types. They learn from their successes and from their failures. They are originals, not copies.

8. *Inspired enthusiasm that's contagious:* Leaders grow enthusiastic as they achieve their daily goals, which are part of a larger plan, not just

daily tasks. They are acutely aware that without this contagious enthusiasm whatever mood they have will also be contagious.

9. *Levelheaded in times of crisis:* These people do not come apart or cry in their beer. They are steady and therefore grasp the needed facts quickly. They know that conflict overcome is strength gained.

10. *Desire to help others grow:* Leaders know there is no saturation to education and that passing along knowledge and growth experiences builds synergistic relations and camaraderie.

Here are some suggestions for taking the road to greatness:

Rate yourself for each characteristic: On a scale of 1 to 10, how great are you?

Rate yourself from the perspective of your team members: Would they agree with how you've rated yourself? If not, why not?

Focus on three points for improvement: Pick out three characteristics to improve in yourself and map out a plan for that improvement.

"An organization quits improving right after the manager quits improving."

☑ Practice Humanagement

Humanagement is simply the ability to use the job to develop the person while having fun in the process. My entire emphasis changed as I stopped managing my people like a herd of livestock and began leading them as people. It occurred to me I could help each individual unlock his or her talent, as well as:

- Set more meaningful goals (personal and professional).
- Better understand and plan their time.
- Use more of their creativity.
- Better handle their stress.
- Feel *safe* pushing their envelope.

If I had an office full of happy, growing people, I thought, there's no telling what we could accomplish. Sure enough, when they began going home at

21

night with their minds renewed and enriched instead of sore, tired, and aggravated, our entire universe expanded beyond anything we would have previously thought possible.

Don't forget the *"while having fun in the process"* part. I don't mean you open the office with a joke every morning. My experience has proven time and again that people who grow and develop and become more capable of handling problems are *happier*. They are happier because they are more fulfilled and actualized.

When employees become more fulfilled and actualized, morale goes up. With higher morale comes higher productivity. I've never seen it fail.

Staff turnover also drops. With low staff turnover comes more bonding and team spirit. High turnover results in suspicion and a lack of personal investment in the job. It's difficult to feel a part of an organization if the probability of losing your job is high. There are the managers who swear their organization has a terrific atmosphere, but people leave because the money is not competitive. There are also bureaucracies where people stay forever, even though they are miserable. A good logo for them would be *"Repeating Yesterday, Inc.: Home of the Living Dead."*

Nobody is having fun in either case. People leave organizations because they're not happy, *not* because there's more money elsewhere. The value of having fun on the job ranks above money. Enjoyable work in an enjoyable environment exerts a stronger hold on people than higher wages in an unpleasant job and environment.

Here are three ways to help get positioned and mentally prepared to practice *Humanagement*:

Decide on ways to practice humanagement: Think about ways you can set a better example for your team.

Rate yourself from the perspective of your team members: If you asked them to rate how much fun they have working for you, what grade would they give you?

Imagine yourself the topic of conversation: If you were a fly on the wall in the homes of the people who work for you, what would they be saying about you in the evening?

"Help a team member grow, and you will receive respect in return."

☑ Cultivate characteristics of an effective organization

These days, the word "creativity" makes many businesspeople automatically think of finances, in the same way that "stretching" used to be something you only did during exercise. But "creativity" here is originality of thought and execution, which are becoming increasingly necessary in today's business arena. Creativity is the power that leads to progress.

When the heat's on, the same old way of handling situations just won't cut it any more. In fact, the same old routines are probably what got you into those situations. Down pressures are changing in nature and intensity. Up pressures are coming from the rapidly changing dynamics of a workforce with a new identity. Lack of originality in thinking and behavior is a sign that you're oblivious to the vise slowly closing.

Any effective organization has an energy you can sense as soon as you enter—even if there's only one person there at the time. The thought might even pop into your head that this could be a fun place to work. Andrew Carnegie, the great industrialist, said, "I've found there is little success where there is little laughter."

When you walk into an organization with low or no energy, you feel that too. It's like walking into a big refrigeration unit: the chill makes you shiver— even if there's only one person there. Some organizations might as well have a sign on the wall that says: Fun is forbidden. Anyone caught enjoying what they're doing will be punished.

Where there is no fun, there is no energy. How long does it take to detect energy or lack of it in an office? Within five seconds, you can tell how much fun it is to work there. Your customers can tell the same thing within five seconds of being greeted by one of your team members.

Change is what happens when you mix creativity and energy. An effective organization is a changing organization. You can't reverse that equation, because it's possible for management to change the look, the staff, the location, and a thousand other things about an organization in an attempt to produce effectiveness artificially.

Change that does not emerge from a healthy combination of creativity and energy will feel synthetic. Creativity combined with energy produces change from within. Changes imposed from outside feel like impositions. Changes from within are self-regulated and guided by realism.

Here are three methods of building energy, creativity, and change:

Analyze the steps used to solve a very difficult problem: Think of one that you or a team member handled in recent months. What did you do?

Consider your team from an outsider's perspective: Learn what "vibes" the average customer picks up when initially meeting any of your team members.

Identify a change you can initiate right now: What one thing could you do at this point to make your organization more effective?

"Team morale and customer service, on a scale of 1–10, receive the same score."

☑ Take steps to grow as a leader

You shouldn't wait to start learning how successful leaders think and act until your boss starts looking for your replacement. If I had known then what I know now, my boss never would have come in and set my pants on fire. I would have paid $10,000 for a single copy of this book back then.

The way others successfully handle pressure can educate you so you'll never have to experience similar situations. Do you know someone who never seems to be on the hot seat? It might well be that while you had your nose to the grindstone that person had his or her head up and looking and learning from other people's experiences.

That means:

- Attending seminars, live or online.
- Reading books, magazines, and newspapers.
- Taking to lunch people from whom you can learn.
- Monitoring your own people for things you can learn.
- Gobbling up audio/video multimedia training programs.

It's not enough to merely study. True learning is the *application* of knowledge. Things get exciting for everybody when successful techniques are put into practice. Keeping all of your great new knowledge in your head won't do a thing to increase productivity.

I speak three to five times every week and there's never been an audience that didn't have at least a few educated failures. Some of them possess enormous amounts of information about the latest leadership methods, yet they're stagnated or failing. When I ask them how many of the new techniques and strategies they have incorporated into their organization's daily routines, they hesitate to answer. The truth hurts. The fact is that for most of us there's a gap between how we do our jobs and the way we *know* how to do our jobs.

How did you score yourself on the 10 leadership characteristics outlined earlier? Now, do it again—as your *people* would probably rate you as a leader. If you're gutsy, you might want one or more of your people who have read that lesson to do the rating.

The score your people give you is the real one. You're only as effective as your people's perception of you. The rating that employees give their boss is always the most accurate measure of effectiveness.

Here are three tough points to consider. You might even want to jot down your reactions:

Imagine your improvement over the past year charted on a graph: If you asked your team members to graph out the improvement they've seen in you as a leader in the past year, what would their graph look like?

Plan your growth: What do you need to start planning in order to grow as a leader in the *next* 12 months?

Think about how you've improved as a leader by handling problems: Pick a problem that your leadership has solved. What did you learn from it?

"Take a mentor to lunch before somebody else eats yours."

☐ ~~Let the chips fall wherever~~

☑ Put the chips back in place

When my boss announced that he was searching for my replacement, I did what any sane and logical manager would have done: I went to the beach. My salespeople needed some breathing space, as much as I needed to be alone with my thoughts, the waves, the sand, and a legal pad of paper. That's where I realized that there was a barrier or fence in my organization, with my people on one side and me on the other. And the fence looked different depending on which side you were on. With this revelation came my first major team-building technique.

Only one factor united all of the people on the other side of the fence: they all hated me. That bond wasn't healthy, but it was strong. I needed to end our segregation.

I could have invoked the power of my position and ordered my people to come over to my side of the fence. But I knew that authority doesn't produce real cooperation.

Another option was to crawl over to their side of the fence and try to recreate the wonderful camaraderie we had when I came on board as the new salesperson. But that wouldn't be leadership either.

Then I realized that I couldn't win over all of my people at one time. At best, I was going to earn their trust one by one. My first thought was to go after the highest producer in the office. But something told me that could foster jealousy among the other team members. The situation could become even more divisive. I needed to win over someone to whom the others would listen.

It dawned on me that the most influential member of the team was not necessarily the superstar but the person whom the others respected the most. Using this new criterion, I rated my team members, from the most respected on down the line. I was incorporating the values of my people into my thinking. The ratings I used were theirs, not mine.

Then, I went to work on the most respected person on my list. Before long, that person was actually saying some decent things about me. Why? Because that person was beginning to truly feel that I was open and receptive to the team's way of thinking. Soon, number two on my list headed for my side of the fence. Then came number three, four, and so on. Once I'd won over about a third of the people, the most respected third, others started heading my way from the far side of the fence. Your people vote every day to decide which side of the fence to be on.

Here's how to get started on the "fence technique":

Determine which of your team members is the most respected.

Identify which qualities make this person so trusted.

Rank your team members in order of peer respect: Keep the list for your eyes only.

"Determination makes failure impossible."

☑ Build a high-performance team

While out on the beach, I laid out a plan. After listing the people in order by respect, I drew two columns.

I labeled the first column *Weaknesses*. This column can get very long, very quickly because we notice weaknesses first and then tend to concentrate on them. You might ask, "Why write down all those negative things?" This list will become a map through the minefield.

I labeled the other column *Strengths*. Then I stared at the blank column: it was as though I had writer's block. Perhaps I hated to admit this person had any strengths. But she was the most respected person in the office: she *had* to have strengths. I forced myself to concentrate on her strengths:

mathematical ability, loyalty to the company, a good sense of humor, an appreciation for the finer things in life, and so on.

Things I wouldn't have necessarily associated with strengths on the job began to add up. I began to realize that the things that made a person strong as a whole were strengths he or she could apply on the job. My focus then shifted from the long list of weaknesses to the long list of strengths just beside it within each person. The old dog was learning a new trick.

Once I realized how many strengths this woman had, strengths that weren't being recognized or put to use in our organization, I was bursting with enthusiasm to talk to her strengths the next time I had the chance. She immediately noticed I was enthusiastic about her potential. I reflected back to her the things she felt were important and valuable. What she thought and felt became my priorities; I would no longer impose my priorities.

We can transplant hearts and other vital organs from one person to another, but we can't transplant strengths. Managers try *every* day—and the operations have *never* been successful. Our job, therefore, is to be a catalyst between their strengths and the way we'd like them to do the job. You'll keep adding to both lists over time.

Do not leave these lists around the office. This is an exercise for you alone. Keep your lists at home.

Each evening, take a few minutes to pick a couple of team members from your chart to connect with individually the next day in a coaching session. Select one or two strengths from each person's lists that you help them to use more in some part of their jobs.

Here are some ways to get started:

Begin with the most respected member of your team: This person is the most influential.

Make two lists for each person: Put weaknesses in one column and strengths in the other. The second list will be more difficult because of the long-term propensity to focus on weaknesses.

Lay out a coaching strategy for each person: Base the plan on your awareness of his or her weaknesses, but emphasize strengths.

"Be aware of their weaknesses, but talk to their strengths."

☐ Leave motivation up to
the individual

☑ Motivate to a progressively higher level

Motivation is the by-product of desire. Desire and motivation can't be separated. They are always at the same level. Motivation, true motivation, can't be cranked up any higher than the level of desire. To best understand how desire increases, and motivation along with it, you must know the three levels of motivation.

Level One: Compliance

The lowest level is *compliance*. Compliance is doing something because you were told to, without much motivation or personal desire. Character is not built at the compliance level.

"Because I said so" is about all of the management ability needed to get somebody to Level One. Simply order the person around as if he or she can't think or reason and has no special ability or investment in getting the job done, other than to avoid being fired.

Level Two: Goal Identification
The next higher level is *identification with the goal*. Identification gives the individual a feeling of investment in the goal and produces increased desire and motivation.

To help people reach Level Two, you must clearly and simply communicate the benefits of achieving the goal. Discuss with them why the job needs to be done and how it is in the best interest for all to do it well. When there is something to gain, people invest more. Many a company turnaround has started at this level.

Level Three: Commitment
The highest level of motivation is *commitment*. There is no greater motivation than when someone feels the goal is truly his or her own.

To reach Level Three, a person needs to understand why he or she is uniquely suited for the task. Show that person how his or her strengths (not yours) can be used to help achieve the goal. Not only will that person feel there is a personal benefit for a job well done, she or he will also bring a part of himself or herself to the job.

Nobody in your organization will be able to sustain a level of motivation higher than you have as the leader. These three activities will help you motivate to the next highest level:

Rate each team member's motivation: Who's only at Level One? Who's at Level Two? Who's up to Level Three?

Find out about personal goals: Ask each team member what his or her person goals are. If they'll work on personal goals, they are more apt to work on company goals.

Coach each person: Use the strengths you now know that each individual has, to help him or her achieve the desired personal or company goal.

"We're tied by straw and think it's chain."

☐ Rest on your laurels

☑ **Continue to grow as a leader**

Right now, I'm extending my arm four to six years into the future and plucking something out to give you. It's the Yellow Pages from the future. For some people, it's the stock exchange index or Dun and Bradstreet directory. For many, it's the company organization chart. Is your name listed? In what capacity? Are you surprised at what you see? If you have a sense of urgency about growth and effectiveness as a leader, you and your organization should be in a prominent position. If you don't, chances are good that there won't be a trace of you left. Your attitude, shaped by your sense of urgency, will be largely responsible for producing the results you want.

Do you have room to grow? What are your team members saying about you at home to their spouses and children? You're not a topic of conversation—you're *the* topic of conversation. When someone comes to work for you, he or she is essentially saying, "I trust you and this organization to do right by me and my family." That is a heavy responsibility. If that person wastes a year or two of his or her life, that time will never be recovered. The lives of your employees should be better because they had the good sense to come to work for you. Your effectiveness as a leader affects people's lives.

A strong desire to do the right thing, beginning with ourselves and permeating every personal and professional relationship we have, marks our commitment to excellence. A healthy discontent for the way things are should make it slightly uncomfortable to sit back and coast. When Walt Disney told his people not to rest on their laurels, it was because he was a leader who understood the consequences of complacency. We should certainly feel pride and a sense of accomplishment when we do a job well, but we must constantly look for new directions and ways to improve and to continue to grow in new directions.

Walt Disney illustrated the need to constantly scan the horizon for growth opportunities when he resisted his advisors' urging to produce a sequel to the enormously successful *Three Little Pigs*. They pressured him and he reluctantly agreed. After the sequel (*The Big Bad Wolf*) turned out to be a box office bust, Disney called his advisors together and announced a new law that is heard around the Disney organization to this very day: "You can't top pigs with pigs."

Invest some time and energy in developing the following three important leadership characteristics:

Develop a sense of urgency: How can you grow as a leader? How can you be more effective—now?

Develop a healthy discontent with the way things are: What could you and your people be doing better? How?

Develop an appreciation for the awesome responsibilities of leadership: Think about how you affect your employees, both at work and in their lives beyond work.

"An organization will never rise above the quality of its leadership."

☐ Promote people so you can pay them more

☑ Find the right manager

Suppose that you will not be allowed to hire anybody for the next five years. Would you rethink how you lead the people you have now? If no new blood was allowed to enter your organization, could you continue to grow and prosper? You bet!

If you face a true moratorium on hiring, I believe you would begin discovering some diamonds in the rough. You will be amazed at the untapped potential in your people if you look at them through different eyes and fully own the long reach you have into their lives.

Your top performers might look at management positions as a way to move up in the organization. There's no doubt that top performers deserve to be rewarded. But moving them into management positions might not be the best thing for the individual or the organization. The mistaken notion is that managers are overpaid and underworked. That's why team members often refer to promotions as "retiring into management."

You might not have a managerial candidate chomping at the bit, even though you need a manager. In that case, you need to go out looking. Henry Ford said, "Asking who ought to be the boss is like asking who ought to be the tenor in the quartet. Obviously, the man who can sing tenor." To determine who has the most potential based upon peer respect, go directly to team members and ask, "To whom do you take your problems if your manager isn't around?"

You're likely to discover that you have a highly respected and well-qualified individual right under your nose—someone who is already demonstrating good coaching and people building abilities.

Your leadership development process should include the following three steps:

Present the realities of managing: Sit down with anyone who is a potential leader and make it clear that managing is not easy. If fact, it is much harder and more challenging than anything he or she has done. If you teach the lesson well, many candidates for management positions will excuse themselves and reconsider the position in which they've found success.

Provide opportunities to show management capabilities: If the candidate still thinks that she or he has leadership potential, make temporary assignments that will place the candidate in a typical management situation. Make sure the assignment simulates a challenge that real leaders must regularly deal with. The way he or she handles the assignment will demonstrate the candidate's management capabilities to both of you.

Evaluate progress: If your company has a management development program, your candidate is likely to be enrolled by now. Evaluate his or her progress in regularly scheduled review sessions. Have the potential manager complete a manager's evaluation checklist that you work out together. More than anything else, keep monitoring his or her continuing interest in making the move to management.

"A person out of place in his or her vocation is only half a person."

☐ Let ~~goals wait~~ when the pressure's on

☑ Set goals when the pressure's on

Come back a few years and picture you and me standing beside my fighter that is capable of speeds near twice the speed of sound. You're about ready to crawl into the rear cockpit for a ride with me as your pilot-in-command. Before climbing up the side of this sleek, needle-nosed, high-performance fighter, you might have a few questions.

The first is "Which way are we going to take off?"

"We're parked in this direction," I answer. "We might as well take off the same way."

"Which way are we going to go once we're airborne?" you ask.

"This direction's as good as the other 359 available to us," I respond.

"How high are we going to go?"

"Until the jet quits climbing."

"How far are we going to go?"

"I don't know exactly, but until we run out of fuel."

About then you will probably decide to skip the flight. "Thanks anyway!"

Many managers try to manage like that and can't figure out why they can't get a long-term commitment from their team members. To build a strong, committed, high-performance team, each individual must be able to describe in detail the leader's vision for the organization and how they will achieve it. Equally important is the vision the team members have for themselves.

The vision we invite our people to share with us is the *future* as it best suits the organization and the people who make up the organization. Helping your people experience the future through their own eyes is critical to effective leadership. Do you know what you're working for? Can you see it in great detail? If you can't, how can you help your people see what they're working for? Helping your people truly see what they're working for is one of the greatest, lifelong gifts you can ever give them.

The great *Mad Magazine* cover boy philosopher, Alfred E. Neuman, said, "Most folks don't know what they want, but they're pretty sure they don't have it." Leading your team blindly without clear goals renders all of your sophisticated navigation equipment useless. Being driven by a sense of dissatisfaction with the present is not enough if there is no clear course established. A clearly charted course or plan is the second-best thing to having a distinct goal. With a clearly charted course, you and your organization know in which direction you want to go. You are intending *toward* something . . . even if the something is not well defined.

Here are three important steps to get started setting goals:

Determine what you really want: What is your vision? How does that translate into specific goals?

Calculate what it will cost you: How must time, money, and energy will it take to reach your goals?

Decide if you are willing to pay that price: If so, when should you start paying the price?

"Deciding not to have a specific goal is a specific goal."

☐ Settle for the old reality

☑ Make a new reality

I did a program once with former heavyweight champion George Foreman. (Even though he is the *former* champion, I still called him Champ.) As we had lunch together that day, I studied his nose from across the table. A heavyweight boxer's nose is a work of art. George Foreman's nose is a monument to goal orientation. It has been sculpted by some of the strongest, meanest punchers ever to step into a ring. I wondered how any man could endure the incredible pain that George Foreman must have endured with so many heavyweight boxers hammering on his nose over the years, so I asked him.

"If I see what I want real good," he answered, "I don't notice any pain in getting it."

A new reality is an achieved goal. We are headed into the future every second, whether we like it or not. We can't hold back time. So, how are we endeavoring to shape the future? What are we doing now that will leave our mark on our future?

Here are my steps to shaping a new reality:

- *Visualize your goal vividly.* Generalizations about your intended goals do you no good. The greater the clarity of your vision, the more focused and efficient your efforts toward it will be. I don't know of anyone who gains value through wasted effort.

- *Break your goal down into doable daily tasks.* When goals loom enormous on the horizon, it's natural to feel intimidated and even over-whelmed. Be realistic about what a human being can accomplish in a day and don't expect any more of yourself or others. Realizing goals is far less dramatic that way, but you will eventually get there.

- *Act on your goals every day*. I'm not suggesting that you work seven days week. But, don't let a workday go by without taking even a small step toward a specific goal. Progress is progress, no matter how small, and the feeling of accomplishment is just as sweet in many small doses as it is in one large one. However, breaking the task down into smaller disappointments will not minimize the feeling of disappointment at never achieving the big goal.

Here are three of my guidelines for goal achievement:

Make sure your goals are measurable, realistic, and challenging: In other words, they should be within reach but only if you stretch and you should be able to know when you've achieved them.

Categorize your goals: Decide which are short-term, which are midterm, and which are long-term.

Set a timetable for achievement—and keep to it: Begin! Don't stop! Concentrate on results! Then celebrate when a goal is achieved—and immediately replace it with a new goal.

"If you don't know what to do on a daily basis to achieve your goal, then it is not a goal—it's a fantasy."

☐ Allow roadblocks to interrupt goal achievement

☑ Overcome road-blocks to goal achievement

I once had a salesperson who was the most frustrating person who ever worked for me. I saw potential in him that he himself refused to see because of a self-imposed barrier. He made $4,000 on straight commission, almost to the penny, *every* month. One month, I did everything but move in with him. I *big-brothered* him to death. He couldn't go to the men's room without me standing guard at the door. I'm proud to say that, in that one month, he nearly doubled his productivity. He made almost $8,000! The following month he made *zero dollars*. The month after that he made $4,000.

I had forgotten that his breakthrough had to be on *his* terms, not mine. When we dug deeper, he confessed that he had never had any more money in the bank than his father did when he was growing up. His self-imposed barrier stopped him just short of ever earning more than his father. Once he realized that he was setting the same standard for his children, he broke through his roadblock—and he was still pushing his envelope at last report.

The following roadblocks might be impeding your progress and you may not be fully aware of them:

- *Team members fear success:* Many people are much more familiar with mediocrity than with success and therefore lack the drive to pursue goals. Fear of success is natural if you have little experience with it.

- *Team members don't understand the goals or they seem unattainable:* If so, examine how you've presented the goals. Did you take the time to think through, from their point of view, their possible reactions to these new goals? Did you break the goals down into doable segments for each person? How clearly did you communicate?

- *The effort doesn't appear to have adequate rewards:* When rewards don't seem forthcoming or consistent with the level of effort required, it's time for the leader to start selling to the team. Actually, the time for selling is when the goals are being established.

■ *The procedures for achieving the goals are too rigid:* Flexibility is one sign of a confident and creative leader. Too many people impose rigid structure on their organizations because they lack basic confidence in their own abilities and the abilities of their team members. Focusing on results instead of methods will open the door for your people to contribute more of their own originality.

Try these techniques to get your people on the road to achieving goals:

Include the whole team in the goal attainment picture: Make everybody part of your success story from the beginning.

Break down goals into manageable, doable increments: Goals that intimidate can become obstacles. Map out the long journeys as a series of small steps.

Frame the goals so that the rewards are clear: If you can't sell them on the benefits for them, you'll probably have to push them all the way.

"Goals are all found upstream."

☐ Let time get the best of you

☑ Plan your time effectively

Most people waste time the same way every day. Robert Benchley was bullish on human determination when he said, "Anyone can do any amount of work . . . provided it isn't what he's supposed to be doing at the time." The following thought was found in the pages of *Boardroom Reports*: "All you can do with time is spend it or waste it. Find the best ways to spend available time and the appropriate amount of time for each task. Concentrate on the best ways to spend time, instead of worrying about saving it."

In a recent survey, business managers blamed their own lack of time management for 92% of the failures among those under their supervision. This raises the ominous question, "How do managers waste so much time?" Several reasons top the list:

- The most common contributor to wasted management time is doing an employee's job for him or her.
- Another cause of lost productivity in management is doing tasks that can be handled by someone with less responsibility.
- It's common to find a manager spending a disproportionate amount of time on a *favorite* or *pet* project at the expense of items that are more valuable to the organization as a whole.
- Repeating instructions is another time killer. This misguided practice teaches employees that they don't have to take action until the boss instructs them for the third time.

Minor corrections can mean major improvements. For example, if a manager figures out a way to save only 10 minutes every workday, that savings will total 42 extra hours gained by the end of a year. That would be like having a 53-week year and would result in one heck of an increase in productivity—all from just 10 minutes per day.

Here are some ways to save time:

Get organized: The average person spends 150 hours per year looking for things. That's almost a full week.

Follow these three suggestions from Peter F. Drucker: Record your time. Don't count on your memory for an accurate assessment of how you spend your time. *Manage your time.* Drucker said, "Until we can manage time, we can manage nothing else." Plan your time, but also time your plan. *Consolidate your time.* Group chores to increase efficiency.

Don't fall for these most common excuses for not planning time:

- "It takes too long" really means "I would rather focus on a day-by-day or short-term basis and just see what happens."

- "I don't have enough information to plan well" really means "I don't have enough faith in the information I've gathered so far so I'd better wait."

- "It's impossible to predict the future" really means "I would have to give up acting on impulse and develop new disciplines."

"Your team members are no better at planning time than you are."

☐ ~~Limit the information you pass on~~

☑ Communicate upward

"What my boss doesn't know can't hurt me."
—The Filter Builder's Motto

Everyone has a comfort zone. There is a point at which individuals become nervous and uncertain about the security of their positions. This is only natural. Losing a job or being reduced in job status impacts a lot more than pride and ego. Throughout a professional career, a person builds a lifestyle that closely reflects his or her professional success: house, car, neighborhood, golf or tennis partners, place of worship, and so on. As a leader you need to understand how much a person's life and lifestyle are tied to his or her position in your organization.

A person tends to become a filter builder over a long period of time with an organization, although it can also happen quickly under the right circumstances. The filter builders know that they can avoid rocking the organizational boat by making sure that the top decision makers don't get upset hearing bad news or by problems they might find disturbing.

If you are a top decision maker, be careful this doesn't happen to you. Make sure the information you should be receiving from the lower levels of your organization is not being filtered.

Everyone has a bigger fish just one link up the food chain. In management situations, everyone has a smaller fish one link in the other direction. If true, accurate, and factual information is being filtered or, worse, misrepresented, as it makes its way through the ranks, the top leaders are likely to be left in the dark about what's going on with their internal and external customers.

How dangerous is this problem? There are some companies we used to hear a lot about and are now gone. They were *filtered* to death.

To be an effective leader, you need real information, whether the news is good or bad. You have the power to fix problems and to help your people grow and develop. You can't do either of those things if you're operating with limited and/or inaccurate information.

Filter builders are everywhere, protecting their backsides. Don't think your organization is immune. You must identify them and deal with them, If not, you are putting yourself, your organization, your customers, and all of your stakeholders at risk.

Here are some things you can do to reduce filtered information:

Develop a mobile management style: Tom Peters calls this approach "management by walking around."

Deal directly with the people around you: Ask questions of your team members and managers at all levels, act on their ideas, and let them know what you've done.

Eliminate filtering: Let everyone on all levels of management know in no uncertain terms that filtering information will not be tolerated.

"Weed out filter builders."

✓ Know the signs of low morale and how to raise spirits

Detecting the warning signs of low morale is only the beginning. To fully address the morale issue, an effective leader must understand what causes morale to fall. Without knowing the causes of low morale, a leader might try in vain to correct the situation and never get to the real issue. Here are some of the most common causes of low morale:

1. People's failure to understand their jobs.
2. Unrealistic or ever-changing goals.
3. Poor communication that can take the form of:
   - Constant criticism (or Big Brotherism).
   - Inaccessible or absentee management.

- Erratic and inconsistent discipline.
- Being thought of as a number.
- A manager's lack of growth as a leader.

4. Over-inflated organizational structure.
5. Over-staffing.
6. Misemployment.
7. Poor psychological work environment.
8. Management that is not people-oriented.
9. Lack of performance appraisal and feedback.
10. Continuing education that is dull or nonexistent.

These 10 elements of a high-morale environment are like primary colors and can be mixed and blended in a variety of shades:

1. Keep jobs interesting.
2. Welcome new ideas.
3. Foster a sense of accomplishment.
4. Recognize special efforts.
5. Treat people fairly.
6. Be responsible as a leader.
7. Offer fair and appropriate compensation.
8. Support personal growth.
9. Promote a sense of belonging.
10. Provide opportunity.

Here are three guiding principles for keeping morale high in your organization:

Study the causes of low morale.

Take immediate action to counteract them.

Make strategic plans to keep morale from falling.

"Team members' morale will never be higher than the leader's morale . . . for long."

☑Value your free time

Leisure time is very important to me for many reasons, and effective time management improves both the quantity and quality of leisure time. One of the most beneficial features of leisure time is the opportunity to recharge your batteries. There is a point of diminishing returns in an overworked individual, and a case of burnout can render a person useless to him- or herself and others. Working oneself to death out of a personal compulsive need is not beneficial to anyone.

To avoid the erosion of morale and a general decrease in effectiveness, I've learned to schedule leisure time for both my staff and myself. Setting a good example when it comes to rest is just as vital as being a good model for proper work habits. Mental and physical renewal are vital components of a quality work ethic.

1. Plan some *quiet time alone* each day.

2. Break tough jobs down into more easily accomplished tasks.

End your workday the right way. The right way is to end on a high note or a point of accomplishment. Doing so promotes satisfaction, improves the quality of your relaxation time, and helps you return to work the following day more refreshed and eager. If you must end your day with an unresolved problem, then write down a clear summary of the problem as it stands when you leave it. Before you leave, clear your desk or work area of clutter and distraction so you can attack the problem when you first walk in the following day. These preparations will also serve you well before breaking for lunch, so you'll get back up to speed more quickly and with less effort after your break. Reorienting yourself after a break requires energy that can be saved with a little forethought before your break.

Work effectively and then take your vacations, all of them. All too often, personal relationships with friends and family suffer because we are simply overloaded at work. This is too high a price to pay for success. What is it all for anyway? I used to pride myself in skimpy vacations until a mentor taught me that I was simply demonstrating my own lack of effectiveness in getting my work finished. Never having time to take vacations is not a badge of honor, as much as it is a mark of ineffective time management.

Take your time and relax. You'll be a better worker, and more valuable to yourself *and everyone else* when you have been recharged. This also means avoiding the urge to turn leisure time into a mini-military drill. Relaxing means spending some time alone and engaging in activities that refresh you and recharge your batteries.

Here are some ways to give yourself a harmony bath (in or out of the tub) and actually get more value out of sleeping:

Turn off the 10 o'clock or 11 o'clock news, with their "if it bleeds, it leads" format.

Spend the last 60 to 90 minutes of the day listening to relaxing music or reading or both.

"Take a harmony bath at the end of each day."

☐ ~~March in lockstep~~

☑ Cultivate creativity

When I took the beach break to see if I could figure out what had caused my office to dive from #1 to #36, I was at a loss for what to do. I didn't have the information then I'm sharing with you now. Even though I initially stumbled across the correct action to stimulate my creativity, I can now recommend such isolation to anyone who is experiencing major problems. Most people in the heat of battle will feel they can't abandon the fight. Believe me, staying in the struggle with no good ideas or anything else to offer won't accomplish much.

The fellow I learned some helpful principles from lost his job as a young newspaper reporter because he "lacked good ideas." His editor back in Kansas also said that he was "void of creativity." Nobody knows the name of that editor. But, almost everyone in the world associates the young reporter's name, Walt Disney, with creativity. In order for anything to become successful (a book, a company, a movie, yes, even leadership style), Walt Disney said that it must have:

1. *A uniqueness factor:* Why should anybody get excited about something that's ordinary?
2. *A word-of-mouth factor:* People can't stay quiet about a positive experience.
3. *A flair factor:* Do it big, do it right, and do it with class.

I think of creativity as the *voice beyond silence*. I've already talked about isolating yourself to experience a clear mind. In the silence of isolation will come the voice that is creativity. Whether or not you are able to induce creativity or it simply happens when the time is right, the following four-step process will help you make the most out of your creative experience:

- *Preparation:* If your intention is to create a new product or method for doing something, it's important to learn everything you can about that subject.
- *Incubation:* Don't rush things. Give a new and creative idea time to cook in the incubator.
- *Insight:* That moment, in the middle of the night, when you sit bolt upright in bed in a moment of insight. Insight is that glimpse at the suddenly clear and illuminated answer.

■ *Verification:* The process of verification brings it all back to reality and begins to establish boundaries.

Here are some basic ways to go about becoming more creative:

Schedule more uninterrupted private time.

Allow yourself to be gullible.

Look at far-fetched ideas.

"Aim for striking originality. It gets attention."

□ Creativity causes
problems

☑ Create a creativity-
inducing environment

I developed what I came to call "imaginars" in place of seminars. These weekly meetings with my managers were, appropriately, held in our district's *Imaginar Room*. While most companies were having seminars, we were having imaginars. A sign hung in our imaginar room that read: "None of us is as smart as all of us."

Our theme was a constant reminder that no one individual could offer as much as the corporate effort of the entire group. My people went in there with the express purpose of discussing solutions to problems and creating new ideas to put into action. Creativity was not only allowed, it was encouraged. Creativity was our first order of business. When we really wanted to dig deep into ourselves for ideas, we rented a room in a local resort and got away from the clutter of daily activities. We covered the walls with flip chart sheets filled with thoughts and ideas we later verified and put into practice.

Creativity Calls for Experimentation. Creativity can create heat. A leader is likely to meet resistance from his or her team members as well as those higher in the organization. The thought of doing something new or different terrifies some people and makes the rest nervous. Yet the leader courageously asks, "Why don't we try this?" The answer is almost automatic from his or her people: "Because we've never done it that way." To me that's just not a valid reason to block creativity. Yet, you'll hear it nearly every time a new idea is mentioned, if not in so many words.

Creativity Calls for Playfulness. An *environment of playfulness* simply means an environment that grants permission to have fun. In fact, it encourages people to have fun with what they do. Urge your people to play the *"What if?"* game and kick new ideas around. Some bosses will catch people brainstorming a new idea and demand they quit goofing off and get back to work. What poor, misguided souls. Their people were engaging in one of the most valuable exercises to improve production, and they were nipped in the bud.

Creativity Calls for Spontaneity. Take the, *"What if?"* mind set seriously. Keep the door to new ideas open constantly. Encourage innovation when-ever possible. I know a retail merchant, Stew Leonard, who started what he calls the *One Idea Club*. Each month, Stew selects about a half dozen employees, making sure every job level and descrip-tion is represented regularly, and drives them as far as two hours away to observe a store where cus-tomers are served well. The next day, the team that traveled together meets and each team member stands up and shares one new idea learned on the trip to use in their own store.

Try these creativity-enhancing techniques with your team members:

Encourage experimentation by praising "success-ful failures."

Encourage playfulness by relaxing old rules of con-formity.

Encourage spontaneity by publicly recognizing new ideas and insights.

"A leader never forgets that creativity is conta-gious and can build enthusiasm."

☐ ~~Avoid problems at all costs~~

☑ **Look at problems as opportunities**

Some good things rise out of crisis. The Good Book says we should be thankful for problems because crisis builds character. I'll go one step further and say that crisis also helps to identify character. Winston Churchill said, "You can tell the character of the person by the choices made under pressure." It's important for leaders to observe how each of their people responds to crisis. Who stays cool under pressure and who doesn't? Who is best at taking the heat and acting effectively to resolve the crisis? Are different people adept at handling different types of pressure situations? Know who is who in your organization as well as your own problem-solving strengths and weaknesses.

Meeting problems head on develops your organization's ability to resolve problems over time. The more you do it, the better you become. This doesn't mean you should arbitrarily allow or encourage problems to develop. Every time a problem is confronted and licked, it should be a character-building education for you and your entire organization. Part of getting better at problem solving is getting faster at it. An organization that has been learning from its mistakes and problem-solving experiences will have a capacity for accelerated corrective action.

A problem that remains unresolved long enough eventually becomes a crisis. A smoldering issue won't get as much attention as a house on fire. If leaders and team members, for whatever reason are unaware of the smoldering issues, there will eventually be a fire to put out. I realize this is quite a stretch to see a positive side to unresolved problems. However, one good thing about a crisis is that formerly unresolved problems will finally be handled.

People who solve problems develop increased self-confidence. The problem itself has an initial amount of power that's proportionate to the amount of disruption the problem is causing in the organization. To resolve the issue so there is no longer any disruption implies that those who attack the problem and defeat it have greater power than the problem. Holding dominion over problems is the substance of self-confidence.

The very existence of a problem or, worse yet, a crisis, indicates that existing methods and techniques are somehow lacking and new methods and techniques are called for. Depending upon the severity of the problem, minor adjustments might be enough to provide lasting solutions. If the crisis is sufficiently threatening, an entirely new agenda might be in order. Crisis calls for something that doesn't presently exist or, at the very least, a different dosage of existing policy.

Here are three ways to turn lemons into lemonade:

Address problems large or small as fast as possible.

Remain alert to the possibility that other problems might be brewing.

Seek simple and straightforward solutions. Simplicity is the ultimate sophistication.

"Conflict overcome is strength gained."

☐ Let change lead you

☑ Lead through change

There are six fundamental phases required for successful change management:

Education	Facilitation
Participation	Information
Communication	Rededication

In a busy organization, you are very possibly involved in several new projects at once. These phases of change management will help you understand where you are in the project.

■ *The Education Phase:* Inform employees ahead of time change is on the way. The *head's up* helps to develop the sense of confidence in your organization I talked about.

■ *The Participation Phase:* Encourage input from all employees on planning and implementation. This bolsters confidence and enthusiasm toward the organization and the project.

- *The Communication Phase:* This is the final presentation on how the change is about to be implemented. A storyboard showing all the final changes can be used in the presentation.

- *The Facilitation Phase:* The change is under way. During this phase the leader's *hands on* participation brings big benefits. Communicating and coaching can only go so far. The leader must get personally involved to demonstrate his or her personal investment in the project.

- *The Information Phase:* Now the leader truly keeps his or her ear to the ground to determine what is working and what is not working. Informal, non-threatening encounters with your people will give you most of this critical feedback. This is when you might learn that proper delegation is not occurring or thinking is still too narrow.

- *The Rededication Phase:* Enthusiasm and energy don't last forever. After the initial hoopla is over, it is important to evaluate and analyze the progress of the new project. Necessary tune-ups and adjustments are made to enhance the improvement.

These three actions will help you avoid the "Other Shoe Syndrome," which results in cynicism in your team brought on by promoting change and not following through:

Focus on how your change initiatives are affecting morale. Solving one problem can create others.

Anticipate doubt. People have natural skepticism that often serves a good purpose.

Never stop selling. Your team members take their cues from you. They watch every day to see if your support and enthusiasm for change has diminished.

"Embrace change. It's saying 'yes' to tomorrow and 'no' to repeated yesterdays."

☐ Keep your head down

☑ Be an island of excellence

After speaking to an audience, I had a manager come to me and say, "Danny, I really want to grow and develop as a leader but the managers at all levels above me certainly don't. What can I do?" I gave this individual two bits of advice. One is that you can't change anyone or anything above you on the food chain. You can't manage the organization above your level, so don't even try.

The second nugget I passed along came from Joe Topper, who was in the audience I had just spoken to. He explained that, because he couldn't do much about changing anyone above him, he had decided to become an *island of excellence* within his sphere of influence. He would get so good at what he was doing that something great was bound to happen. That's the spirit! That's what I'm talking about!

No one is as interested in your career or your future as you are. Take the responsibility of becoming an island of excellence within your present company no matter what anyone else is doing. This will pay off for you in three ways:

■ First, you will become more valuable to your present company. Perhaps even to the point of them considering you indispensable. A sustained high performance record of accomplishment can buy a bright future for you and your family.

■ Second, the better you get at producing results, the more valuable you become to the competition. You are number one. You need to look after yourself and your family. If your employer won't compensate you for what you're worth, a proven record of accomplishment through sound leadership is valuable on the job market.

■ Finally, there might come a time when you want to strike out on your own. Every time you learn and improve as a leader, you become more skilled as an entrepreneur. The more skilled you are as an entrepreneur the better your chances of succeeding on your own.

The ultimate threat to our future is stagnation. Continued personal and professional growth is essential to a tomorrow that will be better than today. The managerial moment of truth comes when you realize that, as the leader, you are the trigger for change in and for the organization. The people in the organization will pay the price in time, energy and money to grow and develop in their jobs as they see you do the same as their leader. The adaptability that will prepare you for tomorrow's leadership challenge is anchored in your personal uncompromising integrity and the other leadership qualities to which you aspire. Looking back over the past ten or twenty years, it's easy to see that the leadership challenges of tomorrow never get any easier.

Here are three things to make you the best leader you can be:

Keep an eye on the future, your own and your organization's.

Never stop doing whatever it takes to keep growing as a leader.

Always keep the growth and development of your team members as your top priority.

"Some of the world's greatest achievements were made by those who were self-instructed."

☑ Final thoughts

"Fear has no strength of its own, only that which you choose to give it. Ironically, that's the very strength you need to overcome it."

"On a scale of 1 to 10, team morale and customer service receive the same score."

"The more each team member learns from the leader, the more they trust each other. It's the birthplace of synergy."

"Great leaders turn lights on in corners of your mind that you didn't know were wired for electricity."

The McGraw-Hill Mighty Manager's Series

How to Manage Performance
24 lessons to improve performance
by Robert Bacal
ISBN 13: 978-0-07-711623-1
ISBN 10: 0-07-711623-2

> Arms you with proven techniques for inspiring breakthrough productivity levels and infusing both you and your employees' careers with renewed commitment and success.

How to Plan and Execute Strategy
24 steps to implement any corporate strategy successfully
by Wallace Stettinius, D Robley Wood Jr, Jacqueline L Doyle, John L Colley Jr
ISBN 13: 978-0-07-711622-4
ISBN 10: 0-07-711622-4

> Provides you with 24 practical steps for creating, implementing, and managing market-defining, growth-driving strategies.

The Handbook for Leaders
24 lessons for extraordinary leadership
by John H Zenger, Joseph Folkman
ISBN 13: 978-0-07-711624-8
ISBN 10: 0-07-711624-0

> This precise, no-nonsense rulebook shows you how and why to focus on your core strengths instead of correcting your weaknesses. It outlines the essential competencies and guidelines for effective leadership.

Managing in Times of Change
24 tools for managers, individuals and teams
by Michael Maginn
ISBN 13: 978-0-07-711625-5
ISBN 10: 0-07-711625-9

Shows how to help your workforce realize the benefits of change and flourish within their new environment and responsibilities.

How to Motivate Every Employee
24 proven tactics to spark productivity in the workplace
by Anne Bruce
ISBN 13: 978-0-07-711619-4
ISBN 10: 0-07-711619-4

Tips for motivating your workforce for their own careers and the long-term success of your business.

Dealing with Difficult People
24 lessons to bring out the best in everyone
by Rick Brinkman, Rick Kirschner
ISBN 13: 978-0-07-711620-0
ISBN 10: 0-07-711620-8

Disarm problem people, find common ground and turn conflict into cooperation.

The Sales Success Handbook
20 lessons to open and close sales now
by Linda Richardson
ISBN 13: 978-0-07-711621-7
ISBN 10: 0-07-711621-6

Outlines a battle-tested program for hearing and understanding exactly what your customers have to say and selling solutions instead of just selling products.

Project Management
24 lessons to help you master any project
by Gary R Heerkens
ISBN 13: 978-0-07-711731-3
ISBN 10: 0-07-711731-X

Provides you with the fundamental skills of successful project management, from understanding the role to working within budgets and leading a team to understanding the basic tools of project analysis.

Leadership Under Pressure
24 lessons in high performance management
by Danny Cox with John Hoover
ISBN 13: 978-0-07-711730-6
ISBN 10: 0-07-711730-1

This hands-on rulebook shows you how to infuse your company with results driven leadership at every level, especially during difficult times.

About the Author

After ten years flying fighters at almost twice the speed of sound, **Danny Cox** turned his need for speed into a leadership system for the business world that transformed a declining organization into a booming industry leader. This high performance climb of his district of offices resulted in an 800% increase in productivity in a five and one-half year period.

He shares this high performance system in convention keynotes, seminars, and sales meetings for organizations throughout America as well as numerous foreign countries. His exceptional speaking skills have earned him a place in the National Speakers Association's Hall of Fame. He is also an elected member of the elite Speakers Roundtable group of North America's top twenty speakers. E-mail him at Danny@DannyCox.com or visit his Web site at www.DannyCox.com.